Star Whisper

By the same author

Unplayed Music

Star Whisper

Carol Rumens

Secker & Warburg
London

First published in England 1983 by
Martin Secker & Warburg Limited,
54 Poland Street, London W1V 3DF

British Library Cataloguing in Publication Data

Rumens, Carol
    Star whisper
    I. Title
    821' .914   PR6068. U/

    ISBN 0-436-43901-8

SUBSIDISED BY THE
Arts Council
OF GREAT BRITAIN

Printed in Great Britain by
Redwood Burn Limited
Trowbridge

"In my ears I heard all the time a sound as a trickle of corn, produced by the freezing of one's own breath into hoar-frost; this music was locally called 'star whisper' and only occurred when the thermometer was below −68°C."

A. Polovtsoff: Wyna: *Adventures in Eastern Siberia*

"There are secrets that the heart cannot reveal to the lips. They are carried to the grave. The willows murmur of them, the rooks caw about them, the gravestones converse about them silently, in the language of stone."

Isaac Bashevis Singer *Taibele and Her Demon*

Acknowledgements

Acknowledgements are due to the following, where some of the poems first appeared:

Ambit, Encounter, London Magazine, New Edinburgh Review, New Statesman, Opinion, Poetry Book Society Supplement (1981), Poetry Review, Quarto, Times Literary Supplement, Writing Women.

"An Easter Garland" won the 1981 *New Statesman* Prudence Farmer Award.

Contents

A Cold Dawn

This is the sky that drank its bitter greenness
from the waters of Gdansk Bay.

This is the sky of the world, its forehead smeared
by the faded sacrifices of industry

and breath. This is the sky
that always shines into my room and makes a picture

of the moment of childish tears after a parting.
The first machinery creaks awake outside

like ice at a thaw. Blind hammers
grow intent on their fathering.

Soon everyone's brain will be working,
shuttling the dark, slickened parts of an obsolete engine.

The Division of Reptiles slides
into the square, announcing its dialectic

to the ship-builder, hurrying
with lowered eyes over the bridge.

He thinks to himself, "Blood fades.
These stains were wept only by rivets."

So the snow-storm of light goes on
filling up the day,

and all the small nos are said
and lost in the monstrous yes.

The Name of Names

Because we belonged to a place of crossed-out names
where letters posed with guns like border guards,
and even the trees, blasted and dead-beat,
quaked again at the thought of changing hands:
because the searchlights swung white corridors
down all points of the compass, and the wire
lay wreaths of twisted crosses on the snow
— and because the snow had lost all track of you —
I returned to the rubbled house that was our home.
Now I feel as if I'll never leave again.

I can't think of the past, the crossed-out names,
the burning stars stitched to the east of the heart,
without distrusting everything I am,
but you could trust words written by the hand
that stroked so lightly back the twins of hair
falling across your frown, their gentle aleph.
I can't think of the future's windswept map,
where trains invent enormous distances
past cities atom-fed, white-hot all night,
past forests black and dense as grammar-books,
without loathing the ruthlessness of time.
But if anonymously you should come back
one day, and learn how near the old place is
— no work-camps, yet, no dogs to leap and tear —
turn and approach softly whatever's there.
Look in the dark that might have been our home.
Among the words that fell from me like dreams
until a kind of liberation came,
you will find hidden, love, your name of names.

Geography Lesson

Here we have the sea of children; here
A tiny piece of Europe with dark hair.
She's crying. I am sitting next to her.

Thirty yellow suns blobbed on cheap paper,
Thirty skies blue as a Smith's salt-wrapper
Are fading in the darkness of this weeper.

She's Czechoslovakia. And all the desks
Are shaking now. The classroom window cracks
And melts. I've caught her sobs like chicken-pox.

Czechoslovakia, though I've never seen
Your cities, I have somehow touched your skin.
You're all the hurt geography I own.

Heart Sufferer

He stands in his kingdom of cloth, the long rolls
heaped in a stifling rococo all around him,
and smiles at the visitors' compliments. His eyes
are calm, however. He is no emperor now,
merely a guide. Business is a small thing
compared to a Bach fugue or even a prelude,
though balancing by day his lost currencies.

He speaks his adopted tongue with a fluent crafting,
except for a few cut vowels. But the poets he quotes
are all Hungarian, all untranslated.
He is recomposing a suite of piano music,
straining across the noise of thirty years,
this business man who makes out an order so briskly
— three metres of small-check gingham in muted green.

His customers tonight are an English couple.
The man beats him occasionally at chess.
The woman he doesn't know. The cloth is a gift.
She presses it to her face, smelling the sweetness
of an orange giving its gold to the treacherous north.
He waits upon her choice, feeling December
creep from the walls, whisper up through his soles.

Here are satiny linings, cerulean
glints from the rarest birds, the earliest summers.
Here are the stripes of crops, a snow of flowers;
and now the flattened cities, tanks, collapsed
angles of aircraft; table-cloths, once dappled
by the Sabbath candles, ravelling up in flame;
small bodies sewn into the colourless dresses.

He turns off the lights (no one else is allowed to,
he explains shyly — it's an old superstition)
and thinks of his tall sons, how they will never
wake the switches of his dying kingdom.
He climbs the stairs slowly, examining
the coats of his two visitors — brash young cloth,
not lasting. His heart warns him, beat by beat.

With luck, he'll leave its music at the door
of his favourite cellar bar. A dish of prawns
is light, easily swallowed. He breaks the necks
deftly, sucks the juice from each stalked head,
and wonders at his sin, the sea-clean flavour.
At pavement-level, London chains its gods
in light; he worships none, but wins each day
by his own kind of fasting and atonement,
time become paper-thin as the map of prawn shells.

The Most Difficult Door

There is an ageing mirror by the stairs
And, next to that, the most difficult of doors.
This is where we live, the home's true heart.
Its furnishings, heaped for some moonlight flit,
Are combs and hats and scarves in slip-knots, all
embodying the female principle.

I sometimes think they must have swum like clouds,
My daughters, through those sea-blue altitudes
Of birth, where I was nothing but the dark
Muscle of time. I bear the water-mark
As proof, but that my flesh could be so filled
And concentrated, heart to heart with child

— It mystifies me now. I want to draw
One back, and this time feel a proper awe
For the tiny floater, thumb-sucking on its rope,
Slumbering in the roar of the mother-ship,
Or let my palm ride switchback on the billows
Kicked in my skin by silvery, unborn heels.

Instead, through thinnest glass I watch them drift
At leisure down their self-sufficient street;
Their territory might be the whole of time
Like that of lovers in some midnight game,
This house their port where indolently they sight
Far out at sea the changing play of light.

Sea restlessness! It haunts the oldest vessel
— A shanty murmuring under a torn sail
That no harbour is safe, nor should be safe.
Only deep waters lend full weight to life.
The maths of stars is learned by navigation,
And the home's sweetness by the salty ocean.

This glass could shine a vista down the years,
Gathering suburban satins and veneers
To a sleepy London bedroom. Hair, long-greyed,
Glows animal; they reach for the delayed
Kiss in the spotless mirror, crimped and pressed
— My grandparents, child-sized and wedding-dressed.

Now it is staring with an older face
— My own. The moon stares too, a steady blaze
of glass-flesh. Through such veils we look at death
And turn our ways of cheating it to myth.
Nature wants children; we, her children, want
A fixed, more moon-like role, a monument.

We've watched the comb reap sparks from our live hair;
Now for the putting-on of mock despair
As timeless as these little pouts and twists
— A rite we go through as the cold glass mists.
We know the brightness in each painted eye
Must often be the brightness of goodbye.

My floating daughters, as I leave I'll see
How you will one day look as you leave me,
How touch draws back, malingering, though the breeze
Of night is tugging gently at our sleeves.
Be wary, but don't fear the darkening street.
I give you this, my opened map of flight.

A Case of Deprivation

A shelf of books, a little meat
— How rich we felt, how deeply fed —
But these are not what children eat.

The registrar rose from his seat,
Confetti danced and thus were wed
A shelf of books, a little meat.

We sang, for songs are cheap and sweet;
The state dropped by with crusts of bread
But these are not what children eat.

They came, demanding trick or treat;
We shut our eyes and served instead
A shelf of books, a little meat.

Then on our hearts the whole world beat
And of our hopes the whole world said
But these are not what children eat.

Two shadows shiver on our street.
They have a roof, a fire, a bed,
A shelf of books, a little meat
— But these are not what children eat.

The Emigrée

There was once a country . . . I left it as a child
but my memory of it is sunlight-clear
for it seems I never saw it in that November
which, I am told, comes to the mildest city.
The worst news I receive of it cannot break
my original view, the bright, filled paperweight.
It may be at war, it may be sick with tyrants,
but I am branded by an impression of sunlight.

The white streets of that city, the graceful slopes
glow even clearer as time rolls its tanks
and the frontiers rise between us, close like waves.
That child's vocabulary I carried here
like a hollow doll, opens and spills a whole grammar.
Soon I shall have every coloured molecule of it.
It may by now be a lie, banned by the state,
but I can't get it off my tongue. It tastes of sunlight.

I have no passport, there's no way back at all
but my city comes to me in its own white plane.
It lies down in front of me, docile as paper;
I comb its hair and love its shining eyes.
My city takes me dancing through the city
of walls. They accuse me of absence, they circle me.
They accuse me of being dark in their free city.
My city hides behind me. They mutter death,
and my shadow falls as evidence of sunlight.

An Easter Garland

I

The flowers did not seem to unfurl from slow bulbs.
They were suddenly there,
shivering swimmers on the edge of a gala
— nude whites and yellows shocking the raw air.
They'd switched themselves on like streetlamps
waking at dawn, feeling wrong,
to blaze nervously all day at the chalky sky.
Are they masks, the frills on bruised babies?
I can't believe in them,
as I can't believe in the spruces and lawns and bricks
they publicise, the misted light of front lounges
twinned all the way down the road,
twinned like their occupants, little weather-house people
who hid inside and do not show their tears
— the moisture that drives one sadly to a doorway.

II

My father explained the workings of the weather-house
as if he seriously loved such things,
told me why Grandpa kept a blackening tress
of seaweed in the hall.
He was an expert on atmosphere,
having known a weight of dampness
— the fog in a sick brother's lungs
where he lost his childhood; later, the soft squalls
of marriage and the wordier silences.

In the atmosphere of the fire
that took him back to bone
and beyond bone, he smiled.
The cellophaned flowers outside
went a slower way, their sweat
dappling the linings of their glassy hoods.

III

My orphaned grass
is standing on tip-toe to look for you.
Your last gift to a work-shy daughter
was to play out and regather
the slow thread of your breath
behind the rattling blades,
crossing always to darker green,
till the lawn was a well-washed quilt
drying, the palest on the line,
and you rested over the handlebars
like a schoolboy, freewheeling
through your decades of green-scented, blue,
suburban English twilights.

IV

In the lonely garden of the page,
something has happened to your silence.
The stone cloud has rolled off.
You make yourself known,
as innocently abrupt
as the flared wings of the almond,
cherry, magnolia;
and I, though stupid with regret,
would not be far wrong
if I took you for the gardener.

Lines on the Shortest Day, to Heroes Old and New

"Since this/Both the year's and the day's deep midnight is."
John Donne *A Nocturnal Upon St Lucy's Day, Being the*
                                                   Shortest Day

It's the year's midnight (I won't count how many
Since your last candle shivered out); now only
        Dust has designs
On the lost She who aped attentiveness,
And clasped your hand, its clever helplessness,
        To Poetry's reins.

So you ride out love's sighs, and history's,
Across the pyromaniac centuries
        To these bright streets.
Hot-line and waveband mesh the stars above;
Down here, the snow grows sluttish at the shove
        Of booted feet.

As for the fact it's Christmas, there's no doubt
In London; neon and tinsel spell it out
        Wherever you're turning,
And though the sun was sepulchred all day
There's a warm flush in the four o'clock night-sky
        Of money burning.

Recruited to our throng, with a lean smile
You press your nose to these alchemical
        Gold-brimming panes,
And deftly lift from each department store
A pocketful of burnished metaphor
        For tawdry stones.

Dear ghost, dissolving inkwards, reinstate
The mourning tongue, the negatives we hate;
    Show hollow plenty
Your whiplash lines whose very commas bite
Until the tears that smart like crimson, light
    Our frozen city

— A grammar for all those who move less freely
Than snow before the wind, or darkness stealing
    Across the floor;
For hungry queues whose meat and bread are doubt,
Closing ranks as the angle from "sold out"
    Grows more severe.

The law in armour stalks their public squares
And rust-thin words are hammered to new powers
    On anvils of dissent.
At home, and tight, we chant a milder verse
To "Peace on earth" (from Harrods to St Paul's)
    — Fine sentiment —

Though not conceded by the governing will.
The West stages its cold-war vaudeville.
    And it's as though
We'd purposefully forgotten being schooled
That here our rulers rarely shoot the ruled
    For saying no.

Between our market-place of wind-up stars
And the gross state with its new breed of tsars
    What's there to choose
But this hair's breadth infinity where you speak
And utter your peculiar heart-break
    Part fact, part ruse?

So Art counsels the self, and rarely fires
A Lucy dead in conscience or desire;
      Yet tyrants fear
That poets are the thin ice of their times,
Their stanzas tiny casements where red crimes
      Brazenly peer.

Be Patron then, upon this darkest day
Of every fierce refusal to betray
      In words or silence.
Bless, if you've power, the art of all that's not
— Exile, and death, and freedoms re-begot
      From nothingness.

13.12.81

The Hebrew Class

Dark night of the year, the clinging ice
A blue pavement-Dresden,
Smoking still, and in lands more deeply frozen,
The savage thaw of tanks:

But in the Hebrew class it is warm as childhood.
It is Cheder and Sunday School.
It is the golden honey of approval,
The slow, grainy tear saved for the bread

Of a child newly broken
On the barbs of his Aleph-Bet,
To show him that knowledge is sweet
— And obedience, by the same token.

So we taste power and pleasing,
And the white wand of chalk lisps on the board,
Milky as our first words.
We try to shine for our leader.

How almost perfectly human
This little circle of bright heads bowed before
The declaration of grammatical law.
Who could divide our nation

Of study? Not even God!
We are blank pages hungry for the pen.
We are ploughed fields, soft and ripe for planting.
What music rises and falls as we softly read.

Oh smiling children, oh dangerously gifted ones,
Take care that you learn to ask why,
For the room you are in is also history.
Consider your sweet compliance

In the light of that day when the book
Is torn from your hand,
And, to answer correctly the teacher's command,
You must speak for this ice, this dark.

Star Whisper

for Eugene Dubnov

If you dare breathe out in Verkhoyansk
You get the sound of life turning to frost
As if it were an untuned radio,
    A storm of dust.

It's what the stars confess when all is silence
— Not to the telescopes, but to the snow.
It hangs upon the trees like silver berries
    — Iced human dew.

Imagine how the throat gets thick with it,
How many versts there are until the spring,
How close the blood is, just behind the lips
    And tongue, to freezing.

Here, you can breathe a hundred times a minute,
And from the temperate air still fail to draw
Conclusions about whether you're alive
    — If so, what for.

A Humorist in Spring

The grey storm-troopers of the wind pour into your rebuilt
city.
They flush out litter from corners, they beat shirts and make
whips of headscarves.
They try to knock down the neo-pasteboard government
buildings,
And tear the trees and fountains from the replanted squares.
You do not admire the cold heroism of resistance, its lack of
humour.
You do not admire the cold megalomania of the state, its lack
of humour.
You return to a country where the trees sway scarcely left
and scarcely right.
Their shoulders shake with soft green laughter. You are
shocked
to read in the papers how fierce and humorless our ships are,
how the young faces inside them are packed like dried fish.
They slice into the sea as the tanks flow into your squares:
these great engines, some say, are the work that makes
freedom.

Museum

Pro bono publico,
Bright wood, clear labels;
A tasteful history
Of sand and fossils,

Motto-bearing plates
And, along one wall,
Like the Apocalypse,
"The Coal Coast" in oils.

Out on the real quay,
Dogs are walked, the flat
Ocean takes a slice
Of sun from the smokeless sky.

The schools line up to go,
But the men in caps
Linger shadowily
Over toy-town mines, dolls' ships.

They get the place by heart
Like the last day at the pit
Or the drawer in the kitchen
Where the strainer's kept.

March, Happy Valley

Days that are finely stretched and luminous
As the paper of a Chinese lantern, keep
The birds up late and whispering across
The valley, where a massive wind feigns sleep.
All down the heath-side, dangerously close
As heart-beats to a foot that wades deep grass,
Hang violets in the strangeness of their blue.
Luggageless, perennially new,
With ancient heads that they can only bend,
They have arrived more quietly than the dew
To feel the perfect cold of where they stand.
The country has a used, dishonest face,
A look of sour back-streets where trade has died
Though half the windows still pretend with lace.
Spring, the sweet spring, is a refugee child
Grown old before his time, a hope displaced.

Regent's Park Crossings

to the "Onlie Begetter"

"It will quite eclipse Napoleon."
   The Prince Regent, on seeing John Nash's plans for the Park.

"Love then and even later was the whole concern of everyone's life.
That is always the fate of leisured societies."
   Attr. to Napoleon Bonaparte

1 Grand Designs

A perfumed handkerchief,
a bedspread of silk, a park.
His sun-sleeked horse carries him,

the seaside Prince,
away from affairs of state
at a glorious, graceful canter.

Taker of air and of slender
hands, he is the patron
of the three-hour lunch-hour.

In his memory, two glasses
kiss in a buried wine-bar.
He has left an art of dalliance,

its lovely formalities;
a path broad as four coaches,
a bank of encrimsoned silver,

drawn swords of fleur-de-lis,
ducks in fancy-dress,
footmen and maids abandoned in the grass.

2 College Fauna

The park is as broad as thought
but the little bridge over the lake

is only as long as my youth.
The students still take to the water;

their slow oars break the dreams of the punting classes,
tangling, braiding the silver hair of Isis.

I set out for Philosophy,
and left clutching Marriage.

How much safer it would have been
to have strolled these quiet paths,

like Socrates and Timaeus,
enquiring, luminous-voiced, into the Why.

Instead, we plunged for the groves
of Discovery of the How.

Yet the lesson continues still
as if it could never be learned

— that difficulty of virgins
with their own nakedness

when love strips *"cogito,"*
from *"ergo sum"* and lays trembling

hands upon timeless fashions, veiled in sighs
and stutterings of leaves, and birds' scared cries.

3 A Brooding of Mallards

The females are crowding the bank
with moody silences,
heads tucked in, wings crossed.

I turn to my imaginary companion.
"Perhaps," I say, "they have heard
that drought has been declared.

"Of course, it's men they blame,
swimming while the park burns,
their plump green cheeks like silk."

He smiles. We walk on
to the formal gardens. There
in flower-light, two lovers

have grown together like espaliered rose-trees.
Slowly they turn to each other
and sink to the gold-haired verge

as if pulled by the weight
of all that they desire.
A nest of differences

is closed with one winged shadow.
I cannot turn to my imaginary friend;
I have made him disappear.

4 Reckoning

At dusk, the May park is suddenly occupied
by hungry lovers. Their hips swing together

dog-like along the dim paths.
The chestnut trees flick little white embryos

at their feet, their feet burn them brown.
Life is always on the verge of a massacre.

Look where the tulips have been pitched
headless, their rigid figures

starved and blade-like, red
smatterings of their flesh

stuck to the earth. Look where the daffodils leaned
to be photographed, each one

convinced it was the star.
They died as they were loved

— *en masse,* a whole generation
of perfectly creamed complexions

rubbished and outstripped
by nature's great law of green.

Now the sky glows the colour of lampshades
in a bistro, the trees are black

crowding big-shouldered like waiters,
priests, aunts, pall-bearers.

Our flustered, red-faced lovers
can't get beyond the *hors-d'oeuvres*. They dip their fingers,

while the chestnut-blossom ticks,
ticks with the sound of a pen-nib totting numbers.

5 Mediocracy

Nothing here is sad or complicated.
The Open Air Theatre will perform
the same three comedies again this year.

The dolphin-boy is a legendary confection,
the drinking fountain, a folly.
The Bandmaster sticks to the light classics,

his shiny regiment buzzing around Sousa,
as if Schoenberg, after all,
had chosen a sensible trade.

Et in Arcadia ice-cream
and billowing deck-chairs.
Each grassy lap is nurtured by the state gardeners,

and picnicked on by the masses.
It's an English Utopian's dream
where the laws (against walking

on certain banks, and fishing
the duckponds) are so pointless,
everybody obeys them.

A quiet, shared happiness bathes
like a sunset, each limited choice,
and only the very few

are tortured by mediocrity.
They are, of course, free to leave
at once by the Golden Gates.

6 Nothing

Your absent presence spoke
softly across the summer
with your haunting absence.

I was between the two,
a child whose timid look,
swinging from eye to eye,

is a metronome of dread,
knows nothing, nothing, nothing
but his guilt-ridden innocence.

So shifts this sea of grass
beneath the wind, until
the sun burns it to stillness

and gold. But what is kept?
The daylight turns its back,
slips the transfigured quilt.

7 Civilisation

This is the made world.
The geraniums are so perfect
they could be plastic

except for their peppery smell,
pure red. The grass has been trimmed
to within an inch of its life.

The roses are better fed
than most of India.
The lake is piano-shaped.

Here are some children, shrunken
in chairs offensively tall.
Manhandled, staked like dahlias

and pushed towards the light,
they sit in on events of movement
with watchful, tearless eyes.

The old nod their heads,
their death-colours suddenly split
by pasteurised smiles, sheer white.

8 Tulips

The tulips parade for May Day
— Galata, Golden Nephites,

Rosy Wings, Abbu Hassan
— all the glorious fighting units,

polished, drilled, not one
man short, happy as sunlight.

They glow like a great flag spread
over a nation's dead.

We admire them; we can't quite love them.
Their faces are hot and closed

as if they had seen torture.
At any minute, we know,

they could twirl in the dandified ballet
of the firing-squad, to face us.

And yet, it must be admitted,
they're a clean, well-balanced lot.

At night they sleep like the guns
of good fascists. Nobody plans

suicide, gets drunk,
falls in and out of desire.

Serene, they have finished with self.
No, we can't love them. But sometimes,

deep in our dreams, they call us
to name our freedom, and then

pepper us not with bullets,
but with bright medallions of laughter.

9 To Construct a Rainbow

Tulips, footsteps, history
unwind long ribbons through the forgetful green.

The trees rain petals — *da mi basia mille.*
The sky is playing at war.

The forces of darkness ride out.
But the sun, great pacifist,

turns a cloud-cheek, shows us
the long bruise of a promise.

I step into the boat;
it rocks on its packed fathoms.

God sends the rainbow love
springing from heart to heart

just once in a while; not for long
may the dull beasts float in such gladness.

10 Phaedrus

The souls of lovers, said Socrates
to his young companion,

can complete their wings only
by embracing Philosophy.

The way hard, these friends
paddled the stream, arousing

a bright complication of water.
Through the hot midday

their silvery dialectic
shimmered below plane-leaves.

Summer wings stirring the air,
love talked itself to oblivion.

They parted not with a kiss
but a prayer, honouring wisdom.

11 Dark Path

Beneath this unlucky white May tree,
we found all we could understand of love.

So we went deeper and deeper down the green path
whose stems grow thickly together like a great friendship,

as if we were dreamed by some old nature-god,
and bound and garlanded with children's hands.

Darker and steeper the green path plunges still,
but now I've lost you; it's late.

Gnats play like little lights above the ghost crowds
of Queen Anne's lace, the lake seems made of dead rain.

What if all that has happened which we named
desire cries suddenly to be renamed?

Here come my two black swans, desultory.
They snap their beaks in the water and complain.

One always in tow to the other, through the seasons
they float their listless epithalamium.

Better, they'd say, an unadoring pair
than one in deep love, alone.

12 Numen Non In Est

The city's ravishing make-up
is all over the sky
in teary streaks;

the sky is hurrying out.
The frightened flowers have sunk
their last coins into moonlight.

A runner heralds himself
with the gasps of crushed leaves.
The breath he unstintingly pours

is kept by the wraith trees;
now they're as lost as he is.
In the clearings are temples,

their pitch roofs low
as frowns. They are dedicated
only to shade.

All winter they'll stand empty
for the dark god has escaped;
his love is everywhere.

13 The Theory of Shadows

It is my shadow I send across the park,
thin as a tree that strives

to paint its name, Japanese,
on a trembling scroll of water.

At night, translucent, doubled,
my shadow haunts itself.

How dim and lifeless the grass.
Men wade in its black borders,

stoop with earth-eaten thumbs
to tool a repeating pattern

they must keep standing back from,
as if the colours hurt.

The baby primulas
lie helpless, muddied with birth.

There are no Forms, no perfections
beyond these sighs.

The world is pure television.
We who watch, cannot be.

The shadow returns across the park,
dragging me by its heels.

14 The Rain and Time

It was the rain, not time,
that drove us from our seat:
rain's fresh, abrupt and sweet

hilaritas, teasing us
with the bookish smell of dust,
the brightened traffic swishing

beyond that iron goodbye
— the gate — which suddenly
had become impassable.

We rushed from tree to tree,
caught not in time but the rain.
All night it stroked the dark,

and this was happiness
— not to care whom you held
while the flickering, whispering threads

held us. And somewhere still
on these dry, forgettable days,
perhaps it is stitched for us

dancingly, in minutes,
our life between-lives as it runs
caught both in time and the rain.

15 Fallen

The sky is leaning and leaning
towards the park, grey breast
suffusing the green with shadow.

The light is crushed between them.
They exchange slow breaths
in heart-to-heart dumbness.

I touch, deep in my pocket,
horse-chestnuts found for the children
and never given.

Dressed in their creamy caps,
they glistened like brushed colts,
silkenly sat in the grass

— creatures of the dew
and a moment's lending;
impossible, but I took them.

Now there's no need to look.
I can feel how the light has gone,
how the tree is dead in them.

They are museum pieces
— old conscience money, carved men
for a game of imagining.

16 Appearances

How like a branch a man
who stands in a high tree.

Blackly he bends on the bending
bough in the blind light.

Smoke rising towards him,
he patiently saws, diminishing

his own margin of safety.
He'd fall with his branch, of course,

in the next frame of the comic,
pursuing to its limit

this art of camouflage
now gathering its echoes

— a moorhen's weed-green legs
— the absurdly familiar smiles

of two who have just met
and share by chance their seat.

17 Clouds

The park flattens.
its perspectives simplify

to a statement of loss.
The flower-lights in their casements,

the lattices, the dark dells
have been drawn upwards, kept

by fat-lipped angels.
Mere blanks remain, an earth

too dumb for questioning
whether life or death enthrals it.

We all wear coats now
— gardeners, bulbs, the sky.

Forgetful snow will fall soon,
blue shadows thicken upon

the burial place, the closed book;
a story told for one.

The Sea Lover

You can't write down what the sea is,
if you've only streets for paper
printed with city dust.
Though you keep the sea in your heart,
you know it's the pocket version
— only a kind of religion,
and won't do for real love,
that edge, those streaming salts.
So, in the end, you give up
and shamefully travel the coast-road.
Even before you arrive
a ripple of cold is born,
and you think without delusion
how the true sea runs to your hand
only to steal and betray;
how it mimes the desolate, heavy
roll of a loveless marriage
that could still resolve you to blindness.
By dusk you stand in the wind,
gazing, your face a prayer.
For the sea will always be more
than you remembered it;
a far, grey animal ranging
gravity's restless cage,
getting ready to come to you, sidling.
You will give it first the dead skin
of your city, the lighted streets,
the bridges, walls and windows.
You will give it your two curved footprints
and your curtain of sooty rain.

Then, with a quick glance back,
because it is hungry still,
you will give it, with love, the sand,
the marram grass and the steps
up the cliff and the road at the top
where tail-lights race like blood-spots.
And, because it is hungry still,
you will throw it your words. With a gasp
the last one whitens, sinks.
What pours through your horrified skull
isn't love or the sea, but the knowledge
of the long, washed throats of the sewers.
Yes, you've spoiled everything,
and everything always was spoiled
but this: you feel it at last
on the tip of your tongue — a silence
welling unstoppably,
cold to its brim — the sea.

Siren

Your children are your innocence, you prize them
greedily, three pink fingers dipped in honey.
At night, three souls slide in their perfect skins
into a rippling length of light. You bend,
damp-curled, still marvelling at the little bud
of abandonment, each tiny, cracked omphalos,
how it is almost an opening that you
might slip into, ticklish, precipitous,
a hair's breadth widening from tenderness
to pain. Sleeked as if by recent birth,
hair cleaves to each small skull, neat as your hand
to well-soaped limbs. So you relinquish power
to babble and disport with the loopy tongues
of child-talk. You have three faces now
with three clean smiles for the mother goddess.
I stand apart, waving a small goodbye,
and noticing that my innocence too has drifted
off with your limpid fleet, just out of reach,
leaving me pure sex, a dangerous pulsing,
a light that sings and warns on the bare ledge of self.

Cherchez L'Ail

London that night was held by golden ropes
   Fraying through the river's black.
The "Queen of Spain" with all her costly lives
Sat tight, as we sat, formal in our hopes,
The bottle on its ice-bed leaning back.
We touched the cloth with bright, impatient knives.

Tides turn, the damaged love-boat drifts away;
   The marriage-teasers walk
The plank, and one in torment almost screams,
But smiles instead. I sniffed my hands next day
To light those flames that stroked our ice-chink talk,
To meet you on the garlic breath of dreams.

Quadrangular

How to unfold the forbidden, scholarly gardens
was a trick I learned today
beside you. I practise it
alone, and a flat wall blossoms
perspective; a lawn,
stone backdrop and domesticated sky,
as astounding as if some tiny
sun-peeled door had disclosed
a casual stretch of marble,
a single fountain twirling
her white taffeta for no one.

To be in the garden at last
is to feel almost faint
with relief, like the right-sized Alice.
The lines drawn
two classes that smile at each other
only through magic boxes
chained to the edges of rooms
dissolve in the merry lattice of our fingers.
While tourists are lectured, we
show each other round.
We'd like the walls to guess
which of us was never young here
— as if they didn't know.
I think they're scared by our mingling
of awe and disrespect
like some lost art of rhetoric,
the tight little problem we set them
by the plus-sign between us.

Afterwards, the light
blooms soft and yellow, forgiving.
On stones ripply-haired
as Pre-Raphaelites, our feet
dutifully part,
and only the page is left.
Here is the miniature plot
where I've laid fresh turves and paving,
opened a quad of words
with solemn, churchy shadows
for you to wave across.

Suicide Fantasy on Carfax Tower

The fivepenny bit wouldn't work the telescope.
It bobbed and swung hopelessly.

I was the captain of some failed spacecraft,
a black hole over one eye like a pirate.

How my silence hurt me
in this soft-stoned, many-leafed city,

so talkative and holy,
even the four o'clock bell

with more to say than I
on the important topic of dying.

Like targets in a video
war-game, the tiny shoppers jerked below

. . . But I was no Kamikaze:
I would time my obscurity

not to kill, but to astonish;
aim for the shifting

dot of the pavement,
not even brush anyone's coat.

How coldly and fluently
the swift air would disown me

but what wild running and ringing
would greet the stones springing

into brain-flowers of white and scarlet
like a mediaeval manuscript.

Cambridge

I am always distrustful of those places
I've never seen in the rain — too much blue sky,
and gilded stone, and young grass for one city.
I envied the legitimate — tourists, students,
structuralists, even the bored wives —
but wrote my sub-text with a scared finger
over the moving sky until it blushed.
Advancing at 100 mph,
the narrative of stern diesel held sway,
and sleeplessness, unemotional
and strangely clear as the aftermath of mourning,
was all I arrived with on that cold station.
I could believe that even midnight here
is sunlit, and that the feasted birds sustain
their small night-music through the month of June.
The hitch-hiker made enquiries about breakfast.
I walked myself in and out of decisions
through soaked grass, thinking *none of this exists
unless I'm here, then nothing else exists.*
It is gathered in one room, its atoms swirling
— biochemistry, ethics, politics
(you know the terms, and that they're never easy).
Bathed and showered in visionary definitions,
I was only ever a traveller back,
glimpsing a lake's smashed sparkles, bright as granite . . .
but then, I am distrustful of possession.
What I have best is always what I lack.

Writing the City

Rhymes, like two different hands joining,
are those slightly archaic correspondences
I look for when in trouble. It's so easy
to start panicking in cities.

All roads lead to each other, sharing slick
anecdotes of combustion. They sell
tin lollipops, barren islands
and the one-way look for city faces.

Things happen and unhappen; cars, like eyelids,
blink their time away. My mind's a city.
That's why I stand so long in the Poetry Section,
and buy apples just to slice them into cradles.

Angel Levine Crosses the South Circular Road

House-fronts flip back like sooty photocopies;
The jokes and quarrels of room after room collect
   On faint-lit glass;
Trying to escape the ultra-violet mutter,
They jam their get-away cars in the golden High Streets,
   Crowding our bus.

It steams uphill, archaic, shambling, at sea,
Fuelled, it seems, by the ache of human breath,
   The dumb, the complaining;
A boy, chained by the arms of his Juliet
As he rides above the warring suburbs, abandons
   Himself to weeping.

And half-way upstairs a Punk Mercutio bawls
"I'll kill the cunt, I'll fucking kill the shit!"
   The film-reel slows:
Three inspectors sway up the shadowy rigging
To display their caps and batteries, schoolboy pedlars
   Of a cheap rough justice.

The kid climbs down, his face a snarl for vengeance.
We've invented this, yet we had no more choice
   Than the rain that spreads
Neon propaganda, or the blood that darkens,
in windows beyond these windows, the small heads felled
   by the just wars.

It can't be true, then, that an iron-black angel
Rose up from a passing basement, and with a sweep
    Of his burdensome wings,
Laid a shadow of music over us, where, as we swung
To its momentary dub of a heartbeat, we found ourselves,
    And our eyes found Zion.

Note: Angel Levine is the angel, black and Jewish, who appears in
Bernard Malamud's story of that name, from the collection *The Magic
Barrel*.

Double Exposure

Come into my room now your better half
has floated off from you a little; don't
mock, don't make a noise, don't spill the coffee.
I'm playing house here, but it's tree-top frail,
so leave your gales and lightning at the door
and come and give me your blessing — what else
are the latest-model modern husbands for?

You can play too — why not become a student
again, and crash out on the sisal floor
of an obscure first-year Philosopher?
Show her some snaps — not of your holidays
or sister's cat, but the future, two giant babies
who come alive and roam about the room,
eating cake and groaning as you kiss her.
The bed looks comfy, but won't give you shelter.
You'll have to find a quieter afternoon
to marvel at the virgin you'll uncover
— double-exposed with baby-scrawls of silver.

Here, where our past and present planes bisect,
it seems quite natural, after dark, to find
the window holds a city and a room,
exchanging surfaces on blue-black film.
Look how the Post Office Tower wears my wardrobe!
A train hurrying out of Euston glides
its amber wishes through me every night
until I pinch the curtains close, decide
it's time for old techniques of black on white.

Above the single bed I've tacked a Klimt.
It's called "Fulfilment". If you'd noticed it,
you might have found it raised a few light questions.
A joke that leaves a bitter aftertaste?

A profound statement on the spiritual
rewards of celibacy? An adulterous comment
or just a wish, perhaps? You might have seen
more intersections than at Clapham Junction,
had you looked up and traced
that gilded dressing-gown with all its scrolls
converging on a decadent embrace.

"If I could tell you I would let you know.
Time will say nothing but I told you so."
— That Auden villanelle makes such a sadness
of infidelity, its echo seems
trapped in all single rooms where stalled desire
throbs like a light-bulb. So what *can* I tell you,
I, whose bed is chaste but whose mind loses
its grip with such alarming frequency
you'd be quite justified in saying it cruises:

that freedom's not like being sent a cheque,
or working after midnight on a high,
or walking miles just for the hell of it?
That mine at least is brimmed with everything
we've ever had and held, and there's no turning
from our history? Since you arrived, these walls
haven't stopped flickering with its lantern-show,
and pictures of fulfilment flicker, die
and are reborn constantly in our eyes.

On a night that's Mediterranean-warm and dusty,
we drift to where the Space Invaders flash,
and street-wise reflexes are newly honed
by the imminent loss of ready cash.
The Camden of stripped pine and antique lights
in harebell shades has locked itself away
to dine. Greek music pours from windows dark
as wounds in scabby tenements marked "For Sale".

The plum-haired sons and daughters of tavernas
gesture like figures on an ancient frieze,
though words and clothes declare them Londoners.

I leave you video-gazing, leave you winning.
Small faces lift for kisses, nonchalant.
I'm clumsy at this weekend parenting,
but no one cries or argues. Back indoors
I add another bookshelf (just a brick
at each end and a plank across), and stack
the comics and Sunday papers that you've left
and that I'll never read — one more sad layer
of history. And then it's time for bed
earlier than I'd planned. (For in the dark
it's harder to see double, hard to see
at all, in fact.) A room's just floorboards, walls,
plaster, wood. And yet it's not the same
now you're not here to tell me where I am.

Skins

There are those that time will carelessly perfect:
Leather, wood and brick fall derelict
As if aware they charmed us as they slip;
This deal table, strung like a harp
With a silky glissando of dark grain
Blooms like a lover from the hands it's known.
Scrawlings of knife and bottle, child and guest
Have warmed its heart, a rough autumnal feast
Spilled into soil, becoming nutriment;
The wood's more deeply wood because of it.
But there are others, the most loved and rare
Time told them once, of which the years despair,
Laughter has scribbled not itself but pain.
Each face is fallen on hard times of bone.
Money will court them first, and then deride them.
There are no masks but sorry stones to hide them.
Yet to the end they haunt disgusted mirrors,
As close as love, and steal with snow-lipped fingers
From little, lying, scented jars each night,
Skins that are pillow-shadows by first light.

Lullaby for a First Child

This timid gift I nurse
as the one clear thing I can do.
I am new and history-less
as the name on your wrist, as you.
But flesh has stored a deep kindness
ready to welcome you.
Take it, a little silver
into your small purse.
There it will gather interest
— the warm, bright weight of you.

North Croydon

A prosperous market-town
put on the fat of these streets.
Repetitive, tritely ornate
like the speeches of aldermen
in the afternoon, they unroll

mile after mile of bay-window
dated as bustles, scraps
of soil where a few ragged wallflowers
drink an acid brightness,
or a motor-bike sullenly lolls.

The rooms slot in like files
in a registry, constantly rattled
by honeymoons or divorces
pending, and, in between,
the wild bleats of the new-born.

Once, in another age,
curiosity was decent.
Only the old remember.
They stare into television,
have nick-names for those they "don't speak to"

— the young, who paint their doors
"Blue Mink" or "Marrakesh"
and hurriedly move on;
those with the darkest skins.
They stand in corner-shops

grown dim and fumy with spices.
It is almost beautiful how
the service is spun out
across counters, a common language
of deafness, accommodation.

The Carpet Sweeper
for Kay Lumley

Mother, last week I met
that old Ewbank we had
when I was three or four,
standing outside a junk-shop
in Bridge Street. I was sure
it was the one because
it knew me straight away.
At first, we were both glad.
We looked each other over.
I think it felt the sharp
impulse of my pity;
it made no comment, however,
and I was too polite
to mention its homeless state.
Mother, the wooden case
was burnished still, and stout.
Its wheels were scooter-sized,
and, just as in the old days,
slyly it urged my feet
aboard to jiggle a ride.
I drew myself up a little
(I'd borrowed your scolding face)
and it apologised.
Ashamed, I turned to other
subjects, praised its lion
trademark, proud though worn;
spoke of the rubber mouldings
that had saved the shins of our chairs
when savagery and housework
boiled in your heart. Mother,
I'm sure it spoke your name.
The sighs of all women
whose days are shaped by rooms
played over it like shadows.

What could I do or say?
I turned, it became small
on the dusty pavement, trying
perhaps to recall the smell
of our floors, the cosy tying
of loose ends, scattered wishes
in its spinning brushes . . .

Israelites

"In a Jewish tradition God was called The Place because all
places were referred to Him but He was not in any place."
                    Charles Williams *He Came Down From Heaven*

When you opened your eyes and gazed from antiquity
onto the new room, the half-born day,

I saw the god of no-place
and the ark of my skull became heavy.

Your eyelashes were little wings — so dark —
distantly flying the broad skies of your vision.

I caught them in a kiss. Your smiles were mine.
For that moment they were mine.

Wake beside me again! I'll stay
in exile till you do,

dragging my years over the midnight desert,
the light I've kept too pitiless to see by.